VALUED

THINGS I WISH MY
mom
would have told me

AVA BLALARK, LCSW

Book Coach – Robin Devonish, Pen Publish Profit ™
Cover Design – Okomota
Editing – Dana Ferguson and Robin Devonish
Interior Design – Istvan Szabo, Ifj
Proofreading – Dana Ferguson
Back Cover Photo Headshot - Chollette

ISBN 13: 978-1-7360071-0-5

Printed in the United States of America

www.avalblalark.com

ACKNOWLEDGMENTS

This book was 30 years in the making but I've only been actively working on it for about 10 years. I suppose it's all in God's timing. Finally, here we are:

I want to thank God for taking everything meant for my evil and turning it around for my good. Thank you for helping me to see me as you see me. I am loved. I am inherently valued.

My husband, Korron Blalark, thank you for all your support. You so bomb. Thank you for pushing me even when I don't want to be pushed and letting me know that I'm capable of everything I set my mind to. I love you beyond words because sometimes I don't have the words.

My son, Korron Blalark Jr., my 1 and only child. My greatest accomplishment and biggest pain. Mommy loves you so much. Thank you for always asking questions and pushing us to the limit with your precociousness. You are so brilliant and even though it makes me sad I can't wait to see the man you become.

My mom, Deidre Turner, I want to say thank you for your love and support. God saw us from the beginning. He chose you for me and me for you. Mother and daughter.

My dad, Michael Pettis, and stepmom Mary Pettis, thank you guys so much for your love and support.

My siblings, Cindrea Pettis and Michael Pettis Jr, thanks for all the roasting sessions because they made me tough and make me who I am. Thank you for your love and support when it matters most. Thank you for my nieces and nephew M'Kailah, Lucas, and Lilly.

My grandparents Matthew and Gussie Pettis, to the best grandparents a kid could ask for. Thank you for the legacy you have left us. Thank you for love, for support, and for stepping in when needed. You two were and will forever be my superheroes.

My grandmother Lillie Mae Harris - thank you for oatmeal on chilly days and pancakes on the weekends! Thank you for always being a place where one could rest their head.

To my best friend Marika Christie Eigege. We rarely get mushy, but as we get older, I think we become more aware of time, how precious it is, and how important it is to let people know how much you love them. I genuinely believe God placed you in my life when I needed you most and we've been rocking and rolling ever since. I love you.

To Ms. Alexis Christie - You birthed my bestie and you let me sleep on your couch all summer of '96. I always felt like your second child. Thanks for taking me in. I love you too.

The Blalark Family - I'm so blessed to get a bonus family. I've always thought that you were all a part of the double that God restored to me. I'm blessed to have a bonus mom and dad in Pastor and First Lady Blalark aka Mommy and Daddy. I get a bunch of sisters and brothers and a whole host of nieces and nephews. Thank you Kemmerin, Keira, Karissa, Kapree, Keenan, and Kammarra! I love you guys. You're stuck with me no matter what!

To Dr. Dwayne Williams - man from the very beginning you were so encouraging. It's been years that I've been seeking your advice and your opinions on this book. Thank you for always chatting with me and not getting tired of me when I constantly harassed you. Thank you for your tips, thank you for your time.

Thank you to my book tribe, you know who you are. I appreciate you all for taking time to support, read my book and let me know your honest thoughts.

Most importantly, thank you for your enthusiastic yes! to my request. It feels good to have the support of your colleagues who genuinely become your friends and friends who become family. Love y'all.

To all the social workers, teachers, and therapists I've worked with over the past 15 years who were supportive and helped me grow in knowledge. Thanks to every student and client who helped me grow as a school social worker, a therapist, and a person.

Thank you, Robin Devonish, for making my dream a reality.

DEDICATION

This book is dedicated to my mother who did the very best she could with what she had and loves me and my siblings fiercely. A woman, who I can honestly say, I hope to be like some day. You are strong, you are supportive, you are love. It took us a while to get here but we made it momma!

xoxo your big girl

For my Grandma Gussie who I love fiercely. There's no one alive who could ever take your place. I never would have gotten this far without your love. I still think of you daily and I hope I make you proud. It's all I've ever wanted to do.

Love Fuji ♡

CONTENTS

Welcome to my journey of self-awareness, self-management and social-awareness, responsibility, relationship building and decision making.

INTRODUCTION

"Slow down baby girl. You'll get there."
– Ava Blalark

I wish present-day me could tell younger me to "slow down baby girl, you'll get there." That is the advice I would have given myself if I could go back in time. That is the advice I wish my mother had given me. As much time as I spent wanting to be an adult to do things my way, I wish I had spent more time understanding the things going on around me, how they might shape me in the future, and speaking up about them. But you don't think about those things as a kid. In fact, sometimes, you don't think about those things as an adult. Have you ever looked in the mirror and asked yourself: "Why am I like this?" Whatever "this" is? Have you ever felt anxious or unfulfilled? Maybe you have had difficulty in relationships with family or friends. These were all my experiences. For me it was, and sometimes still is, insecurity and dealing with conflict. It's sometimes having a hard time showing up for people that I care about. Whatever "it" is, you can work through it as well. No matter where you are in life - you can begin to write your own narrative. You may not have written the introduction, but you can certainly finish the story. There's no time like the present to get started. Let me be clear, I have not arrived. This journey is a process and all that matters is that you make progress. Commit to the journey and you'll do fine.

As a girl, as a teenager, and even as a young adult, I remember feeling awkward in my skin, as if I just didn't know how to wear it - I was uncomfortable in my own body. I was too tall (taller than most of my friends) too skinny, with teeth that were too big. I hated my smile because of the gap in between those 2 big front teeth. The gap I inherited from my father and the big teeth from my mom. Best of both worlds, I guess. Any time I would smile my right hand would usually go up to hide those teeth. I had glasses with lenses so thick I

1

could see into the future since the 9th grade because I spent all of elementary and middle school straining to see the board from the back of the class. I'm just going to say it. I felt ugly. I'm not saying I was ugly, but I felt ugly. I thought I was ugly. What I have learned is that sometimes the negative thoughts that we think are stronger than reality. What I've just described would be a stark contrast to the woman I am today. I'm still tall, but I relish in it. I'll wear a five-inch heel on my best day which puts me well over 6 feet. While I may have put on a few pounds most would still consider me slim. I've put on more than a few so you can imagine just how skinny I was back then and being skinny was not the thing to be in my neighborhood when I was growing up. Growing up in an African American family being thin wasn't always considered attractive. My family would make comments about having "big ol' pretty legs" while I was called "big bird" and "tree trunk" by family members. They did it lovingly, but it still reminded me that I was tall, skinny, and awkward. The boys also wanted someone who was a little curvier with big legs and an even bigger behind. I remember helping my older cousin peel off layers of tights and leggings that she would wear to school every day to appear curvier in her jeans. She would lay on the bed and I would grab one pant leg and my cousin would grab the other and we would yank and pull those layers off each day only for her to shimmy her way into each layer the next day. I took those expectations right into young adulthood and college. Imagine the university nutritionist's surprise when I made an appointment asking how I could quickly put on 15-20 pounds in my freshman year of college. Even today, television, music, and your favorite Instagram models will have you believing that you have to have big breasts, a small waist, and a butt as big as Nicki Minaj's to be attractive.

So again, imagine a tall, skinny, awkward girl with thick glasses and huge teeth and you've got a recipe for low self-esteem. Fast forward some and you'll find that contacts replaced the glasses. My teeth are the same size, but braces fixed the gap along the way. I feel better about the way I look on the outside and I love showing off my smile even though sometimes I'm concerned that I'm showing too much gum. Trust me, it's always something.

Value Gained

I wish I had known that real self-esteem doesn't come from fixing the outside. That is a work that needs to be done on the inside. You can improve the outside, but if you don't face your fears, insecurities, and what is going on inside your head, it won't work. What voice do you hear and what is it telling you? Who are you? Is that your idea or someone else's? I've seen beautiful girls struggle with their physical appearance. I've seen smart people question their intelligence. I've seen competent people second guess their ability. You've seen it too. Whose voice are they listening to? Most times it's the voice that is the loudest and strongest. Maybe it comes from family, maybe it comes from friends, or social media. You have to find the small quiet voice and strengthen it.

I wrote a note to myself in May of 2019 about inherent value. I'm not sure where I was or where I heard it, but it struck me, and I jotted it down. Next to those two words I wrote (or rather typed in my iPhone) "do I deserve the best?" Webster's dictionary defines inherent as 'involved in the constitution or essential character of something: belonging to by nature or habit'. So, just by nature you have value. You have worth. That value is built in, organic, inseparable, and deeply rooted in you.

So, to the question "do I deserve the best?" The answer is: Yes. Yes, I do. Yes, you do. Just because you are. So, what are you going to do about it?

Keep this in mind; everything you are experiencing right now shapes the woman you will become. (And if you happen to be reading this and you are well past your teenage years, everything that you have experienced has had a hand in shaping the woman you are.) Every experience will change how you view the world around you and how you will respond the next time something similar comes your way. Embrace that you will never stop growing as a woman, never stop changing, never stop learning something new about yourself. Live in and embrace the moment. Think about how your experience may affect you and most importantly, how you can find the value in it to make it work for you and to help someone else. You can turn your experience into your evolution. You can turn your pain into purpose. Out of the silence find your voice.

I want to share with you how I found my voice when I thought I had lost it. I wrote my truth when I was too afraid to speak and found my value in the place I never thought to look – myself. I want to show you how to use social and emotional learning or SEL to become more aware of the impact trauma and other events have on your life. And even though SEL wasn't a thing when I was growing up, this process through which we understand and manage emotions, set and achieve positive goals, feel and show empathy for others, establish and maintain positive relationships, and make responsible decisions (CASEL) hold true then and now. I hope that you see these 5 skills: self-awareness, self-management, social awareness, relationship skills and responsible decision-making skills as they show up in my life in every story I tell. But more than anything, I hope this book is a journey of self-discovery for you.

Journal Prompt:

What messages did you or do you receive from your parents, caregivers, and others about who you are? How did these messages affect your identity and self-esteem?

Now that you've been introduced to the idea of inherent value, what do these words mean to you? Do you believe you deserve the best? Begin to strengthen that voice and write about your inherent value.

_____

_____

_____

_____

_____

_____

_____

_____

_____

_____

_____

_____

_____

_____

_____

_____

_____

Write a letter to yourself five years in the future. Tell her about your hopes, dreams and what you want to accomplish. Talk to her about something you're struggling with and how you plan to get through it so that you can accomplish those things. Give her a piece of advice.

_____

_____

_____

_____

_____

_____

_____

_____

_____

_____

_____

_____

_____

_____

_____

_____

_____

_____

Now, write a letter to yourself to be opened in one year. Write down at least three short term goals and three actions steps to how to get there. In six months take a look at your goals. Check to see if you are on the right track to achieving your goal or do you need to revise your action steps.

_____

_____

_____

_____

_____

_____

_____

_____

_____

_____

_____

_____

_____

_____

_____

_____

_____

_____

_____

Self-Awareness

CHAPTER 1
MIRROR–MIRROR

I recently discovered a quote by James Baldwin: "Not everything that is faced can be changed, but nothing can be changed until it is faced." This quote spoke volumes to me because it is how I'd like to say I live my life now. Through years of soul searching, some tough life lessons, and a little bit of therapy I can accept what I cannot change and face, head on, the things I can. I don't live in fear of bad things happening because this is life and I know life happens. I believe I'm strong enough to face anything that comes my way even if I feel like I can't. It is a continuous process. I started seeing my therapist in 2017. I was in a good place in my life (job, marriage, kid, etc.) but I still felt alone. I still felt unhappy when I thought I should be happy. I was still struggling in my relationships. Even though people tend to like me, I didn't feel like I was making real connections. I had a job helping people, but I needed to help myself. I remember after a particular therapy session I told my dad, "I'm trying this new thing where I tell people how I feel." To which he replied, "Yeah"? He proceeded to tell me that when I was younger and things would happen, he would continuously ask me how I felt to which I would respond, "Fine, I'm fine." Little did I know that this "I'm fine" or some variation of the phrase would become my mantra later as an adult. "It's okay, I'm fine." "It's cool." "I'm good", I'd say, even when I wasn't. Do you ever find yourself saying you're okay when you're not? At some point I decided that was not enough. I needed to speak the truth about how I was feeling but something was holding me back. I noticed that I started to feel anxious to talk about how I was truly feeling. I also felt like a burden and I didn't want to unload my feelings on other people.

To become the woman you want to be, you must take a good, long and hard look in the mirror and face you. Not everything about you can be changed.

You can get braces or Lasik eye surgery, but there are things about you that you must to deal with. You cannot change who your parents are. You cannot change the decisions they make even when those decisions affect you. You cannot change certain situations you find yourself in. You cannot change the past. You cannot predict the future. What you can change is how YOU view situations. You can change how YOU respond to something. You can work on YOUR healing. However, you can only change these things once YOU decide to face them.

While I love James Baldwin's quote, as a kid, the quote I lived by was "There's no use in crying over spilled milk." Another personal favorite was "you have to play the hand you're dealt.' What kind of motto is "play the hand you're dealt" for a kid? A kid born and raised on the west side of Chicago - that's who. A kid who grew up playing spades and knows it's bad form to just throw in your hand. You must play it no matter what even if you know you're going to lose that round. You know who lives by that motto? A kid who has experienced homelessness, witnessed domestic violence, divorce, parental incarceration and more. When I say I have an idea of what you may be going through I mean it. At the time I wouldn't allow myself to cry over the spilled milk. I wouldn't allow myself to throw in my cards. And while I thought those life mottos got me through, I was missing something important, something that would affect me for a long time. It would affect my relationships with others but more importantly, my relationship with myself. That simple truth was if you can't be honest with yourself, you'll never be able to be honest with others.

Instead of facing things, I often hid from them, buried them, and smiled even when I didn't feel like smiling. In my mind, at the time, that meant there was no time to cry about things I could do nothing about. That meant that if someone asked me if I was okay, I would always say "yes" because what could they do about it? What would saying how I felt accomplish? It would only suc- ceed in making the people around me feel uncomfortable, which would make me uncomfortable. I knew my parents had a lot going on and I did not want to be another worry on their list. They never told me I was a worry or a bother; it's just how I internalized things that were happening around me. I had to look out for me, because at the time, I didn't think they were capable of doing it. I know so many of you are doing the same thing: holding in your own pain while taking on the burden of others. So, as the saying goes, "there's no use in crying over spilled milk." Tell them you're fine (or some variation of the sort). Clean up the milk, erase the evidence that it was ever there, and keep it moving.

Value Gained

I rarely, if ever, heard my mom complain or simply express her feelings about a situation. I think I got the idea that there's no use in crying over spilled milk from her. If she complained, cried, or screamed alone I never knew it. I don't consider it a weakness; it's a quiet strength she exudes but still, I wish my mom had told me to use my voice. I wish I had known that it's okay to cry over spilled milk. You have a right to say I am hurt, I am sad, or angry about what has happened even though you can't change what happened. Expressing how you feel is not about getting another person to change or changing the situation. Saying how you feel is about you. It's learning how to identify what's going on inside you and communicating it to someone else. When you become self-aware you can understand how your feelings, thoughts, and behaviors are working together to influence you. Being self-aware isn't as easy as it may seem especially if you're still learning who you are.

What happens to someone who doesn't cry over spilled milk? What happens when you just keep playing the hand you're dealt? You become closed off to the people who matter most. You build a wall to protect yourself. For a long time, I didn't know how I felt most of the time. I really believed I was fine even when I was not. I hid true feelings so well that they became hidden from me. All I knew is that I would feel off - my heart would beat fast; my breathing would become shallow and I would have an overwhelming sense of dread. That still happens sometimes but now I can put an emotion to the physical sensation. Is it anger, fear, anxiety, sadness? If you can't identify it, you certainly can't learn to cope with it. Believe it or not, I still have a difficult time labeling emotion and what I have found is that many people have that same difficulty, but it's nothing that a little practice won't help.

Remember it's okay to cry over spilled milk and feel angry because it's all over the floor. It's okay if you're sad or anxious about the clean up. It's even okay if you feel happy about it. Say how you feel about it. Then, and only then, can you begin to clean it up.

You can play the best you can with the hand you're dealt AND declare that this is a shitty hand you've been dealt. But also know that the game is not over and there is still playing left to do. We play to win, not just to survive.

Journal Prompt:

If you could create a quote that you currently live your life by, what would it be? Why did you choose this quote?

_____

_____

_____

_____

_____

_____

_____

_____

_____

_____

_____

_____

_____

_____

_____

_____

_____

_____

_____

_____

Are you happy with your life's quote? If not, take a moment to think about what quote you would like to live your life by.

_____

_____

_____

_____

_____

_____

_____

_____

_____

_____

_____

_____

_____

_____

_____

_____

_____

_____

_____

Self-Management I

CHAPTER 2
CHECK YOURSELF

If you don't have anyone you can trust sharing your spilled milk with, write it down. One of my saving graces was the gift of a journal. It was given to me by a woman named Diane on July 5, 1995. I was 12 years old. I'll never forget it because I wrote it down. There were not many people I trusted when I was younger, and I needed to get what I was thinking about what was happening around me out. Writing has always been a way of escape for me. I remember journaling at 10 and 11, but lost my previous journal in one of our many moves as a child. But, the one Diane gave me, I still have it and I'll share some things from it with you. Diane was a woman who lived in the same shelter we lived in (I'll tell you more about that later). I remember talking to her as she cleaned out some of her things and came across this blue marble hardcover journal. She asked me if I wanted it and I eagerly replied yes! My first entry is dated July 4, 1995 because even though I got it on the 5th I wanted to talk about the 4th of July holiday. The first paragraph reads:

"Well if you don't know we live in a shelter for the time being and we should be outta here by August, maybe even by the end of July. It's not so bad here though. In fact, it's not bad at all except for the roaches. Everyone gets their own bed, and you can buy your food. You can do practically anything you want to."

This has to be one of the earliest examples of me not crying over spilled milk. I hated living in that shelter. I know that for a fact. By the time I had written that it wasn't so bad we had already been there a few months and would continue to be there another month or so. I never told my mom how much I hated it because I didn't want to make her feel bad about our situation. I know that that experience changed me forever.

For as long as I can remember we have always lived with someone else. For a moment in time my parents were married and lived together. I think it started okay but quickly turned sour. I mean don't all relationships start off good? They were young. They met in high school. They had me by the time my mom turned 21 and my dad was 22. They got married shortly after I was born. It was a marriage plagued with infidelity, physical abuse, and drug use. It probably lasted longer than it should have but it still turned our world upside down. I was about six years old and what I remember most were the black garbage bags at the door. My life and the lives of my sister and baby brother were thrown into huge black garbage bags to be carried to the next place. How do you fit your life into garbage bags? All of your clothes, all of your toys? You can't fit the pink bike with no training wheels that you got for your 5th birthday into a garbage bag. You can't fit memories into a garbage bag. I didn't want to leave our 2-bedroom apartment behind. I didn't want to leave the bunk beds and the room I shared with my little sister. I tried to hold on to the memory of getting my hair relaxed for Easter in the kitchen or looking out the living room window onto the busy street below. But we were leaving, never to return and our living situation would not be stable again for years to come. We traveled, with our black garbage bags to the only place we could go I imagine - to Granny's house. She is my maternal grandmother. She did and still does own a 2-flat building on the west side of Chicago. She, her husband at the time, and her son lived on the 1st floor. On the second floor, in a 3-bedroom apartment, lived my mother, her four sisters, and all their children. So, imagine five adult women and about 11 children living in a 3-bedroom apartment. I'm not quite sure how we did it, but we did, for years. My siblings and I shared a room with my mom. We slept on a mattress on the floor - the four of us. There was a television in the corner. There was one window directly across from the door that overlooked a neighbor's brick wall. The walls were bare but my mom kept it clean. I've never asked my mom how she felt about that because I assume it was hard. What I do remember is running around the living room with my cousins having a blast. I remember when we all caught chicken pox and had to be rubbed down with pink calamine lotion. I remember my grandmother making large pots of oatmeal for breakfast before school and if we were lucky, pancakes on the weekend.

Everyone in my family lived with granny at some point in their life. We were back and forth there for the entirety of my childhood. We would find another place for a while, but we always ended up back there. We 'graduated' from the 2nd floor to the 1st floor with granny when she and her husband divorced. Then we moved to the basement. I won't even try to create a timeline of all the places I've lived because I can't make sense of it all in my head. My mother and father would briefly rekindle their love throughout the years until officially divorcing when I was in 5th grade. We lived with my paternal grandfather for a while. (I believe it was a little bit of 2nd grade, 3rd, 5th, and 6th grade). We lived at granny's in between those times. My mother and grandmother would get into it and we would have to leave. That's how we ended up in the shelter. It was in 7th grade. I'm not sure what they argued about, but my mother packed up me and my siblings and we went to my great grandmother's house. My great grandmother lived in an assisted living facility for seniors so children were not allowed. Now, it was the four of us crowding my great-grandmother in her tiny 1-bedroom kitchenette style apartment. We would get up each morning and head to school from the senior's building saying hi to all the old folks on our way out. It was only a matter of time before we were caught. The property managers called the police one day and told my mom we had to go, or my great grandmother would have to go. Since we had no other options we ended up at the shelter. The day we got there I remember being shocked at the enormous room filled with bunk beds. Dozens of bunk beds lined the concrete floor with no partitions or privacy for families. Living with my aunts and cousins had been crowded but at least they were family. This was a place full of strange people and strange things. We were shown around a small cafeteria style room with a refrigerator filled with food with people's names written all over it. Next, the bathroom, with showers and toilets lining the left side and sinks on the right side. You would need to wake up early to beat the rush or risk being late to wherever you needed to go. We met some of the other families and the people seemed nice – just people, like us, who had found themselves in an unlikely predicament. Once again, all of our belongings were stuffed into black trash bags. Oh yeah, this was by far, much worse than living in that apartment with my aunts and cousins. I also wasn't six years old. I was 13 at this point and I knew this was not the way it was supposed to be. As we made our way to our bunks, I remember feeling scared and unsure of our future. How long would we be here? Would my dad or my other grandparents rescue us? I was frightened and my mother had no real answers for us. The very first night there I cried for what seemed like an eternity until sleep finally rescued me. I woke up the next day with my eyes swollen from crying so much. I woke up wishing it was all a dream. It wasn't a dream; it was a nightmare. Imagine my surprise when nights turned into weeks and weeks into the months. We spent the rest of the school year and the entire summer of 1995 in that place. Each day was a little easier but that first night was the worst. Even though I had been crying all night, I still wanted to go to school when I woke up. We had our 7th grade field trip to play laser tag for winning the "penny wars" at school. But our lives were in shambles. How would I get to school? How would I get back to the shelter? I guess at some point we figured it out but not that day. I missed the field trip that I waited for all year.

After that spring and summer in the shelter we ended up right back at granny's house, and for the life of me I couldn't figure out what the entire point had been to begin with. Even after that experience, we still couldn't quite figure it out. Between 8th and 10th grade, I lived with my father, paternal grandmother, paternal aunt and uncle, and maternal great grandmother who I helped take care of. I lived on the South side in an apartment my mom shared with her boyfriend, with that boyfriend's sister, and with my best friend on the North side of Chicago. In two years, I had lived in seven different places. By 11th grade we were back with granny until I went away to college at the University of Illinois.

Value Gained

I wish there were an explanation for why we kept moving. I mean I had my suspicions (the drug addiction, failed relationships, and so on.) At the very least I wish I had known that while things were tough it would get better. My mother was doing the best she could and that would just have to be enough.

What happens when a child with no real stability becomes an adult? They may become unstable and mimic their childhood OR they become rigid in their quest for stability. It is more of the latter for me. It became increasingly important to me to have a career, a family, and buy a home. I wanted to have my child or children attend the same school, grow up with teachers who knew them, and develop lifelong friendships. Deviations from this plan caused great anxiety as I scrambled to have a plan A, B, and C to deal with any problems that might come my way. It also made it exceedingly difficult for me to be decisive because I was always afraid of making the wrong choice and that the wrong choice would change the trajectory of my life for the worse somehow. What I had was never enough, I was always striving for something more, never satisfied and enjoying what I have.

I wish my mother had told me that life is full of surprises. Things won't always go as planned and sometimes you have to roll with the punches. With all the changes in our life maybe she did teach me this in her own way. She certainly rolled with the punches but she coped in unhealthy ways. And then I learned to cope in unhealthy ways. While my vice would never be drugs and alcohol, my need for perfection and constantly chasing a goal was weighing heavy on me. It's okay to have a plan. I suggest having a backup plan but it's much more important to live life day by day. Make sure you stop to enjoy your accomplishments, and when difficulties arise remember that you have the strength to get through them. Look at what you've gotten through already. "For now," is a small phrase that I have come to love. The only thing constant in the world is change; however, you can make the best choices "for now". "For now," doesn't mean forever because we can't predict the future. For now, I am making the choices that suit me where I am in my life today and that I think will suit my future. If it doesn't work out as planned for some reason, I will make new decisions that will fit that time. I am confident that I will be able to handle whatever life throws my way.

Journal Prompt:

What is a painful situation that you have dealt with in the past or that you are struggling with right now? What effects did/does it have on you?

_____

_____

_____

_____

_____

_____

_____

_____

_____

_____

_____

_____

_____

_____

_____

_____

_____

_____

_____

_____

Talk about how you feel or felt about the situation. How did you cope? What healthy ways can you choose to cope with the difficulty?

_____

_____

_____

_____

_____

_____

_____

_____

_____

_____

_____

_____

_____

_____

_____

_____

_____

_____

_____

_____

_____

_____

Remember you are not broken. You are still here! How can this experience help you to evolve?

_____

_____

_____

_____

_____

_____

_____

_____

_____

_____

_____

_____

_____

_____

_____

_____

_____

_____

_____

_____

_____

There are so many ways to help regulate your emotions. Everyone is different and not everything works for everyone. I love to use deep breathing to help me regulate and calm down. Nothing fancy; I just close my eyes and take slow deep breaths, in through my nose and out through my mouth. Other ways to manage your emotions or painful situations include the following:

- Journal (another favorite of mine)
- Meditate
- Go for a walk
- Exercise/Yoga
- Count to 10

If you have a smart phone, go to your app store and search mindfulness - choose an app (most have a free version) to help you get started.

Relationship Skills I

CHAPTER 3
GOOD FIGHTING

A relationship is a bond or a connection between two people. It can be a romantic relationship, one between family members or a friendship. As human beings we were meant to be connected to others. We weren't meant to do life alone but that doesn't make relationships easy. They take work, they take effort, they take energy. Casel (2020) describes relationship skills as maintaining healthy and rewarding relationships with diverse individuals and groups. The ability to communicate clearly, listen well and cooperate with others. It is the ability to negotiate conflict and seek and offer help when needed. It is an important skill to learn. I think relationships help us to see ourselves for better or for worse. In the right relationship, the mirror is held up for you to examine yourself and become better.

The first relationship you see is the relationship between your parents or the lack thereof. I could not tell you when it started or if I noticed a change in my parents but at some point, I knew something was wrong. I knew they were into some bad stuff. At some point in my life, I will say both my parents had a drug addiction problem. Anyone who knows them, knows that to be true. They will tell you themselves (my dad is a little more vocal than my mom about it). I'm sure it had a hand in destroying their marriage. It prevented them from being fully present in the lives of myself and my siblings as children. My parents' drug use created my extraordinarily healthy and sometimes unhealthy fear of drugs. I don't know what it takes for someone to become addicted. Does it happen after one use or several uses? I'm not sure because everyone is different. I was sure of the effects on our family so I never wanted to find out. One of those effects being that it turned my gentle father into an angry man at times.

I was five years old the first time I remember it happening. That would mean my sister was around three years old and my brother was just a baby. I know it wasn't the first time it happened, however, it's the one time I remember most. Daddy (in Chicago we pronounce it "Deddy") threw a shoe and hit my mom in the eye. The shoe was a tan, open toed heel. That's what I remember. I don't know which part of the shoe hit her, but her eye swelled up and turned black and purplish on my mother's light brown skin. There was lots of yelling and screaming and crying. Everyone was crying - Mom, dad, me, my sister, and the baby. Why was this happening? What had momma done to deserve this and why was daddy so mad? I remember being scared but not for myself. I was not afraid that my father's wrath would turn on me. He would never hit me like that. I can count on one hand how many times my dad ever even spanked me. I was scared for my mom. I could tell the physical pain was excruciating and while it may have only been a moment, it seemed like it was going on forever. I had no idea of the emotional pain and scars that these events would leave behind. Not only on my mother but also on the two little girls who watched it happen right down to the baby boy who could probably feel the house's tension. These events would shape our relationships with significant others. It would affect how we deal with conflict and maybe even things I haven't begun to put my finger on.

My brother and I are remarkably similar in our approach to handling conflict in relationships. We can be a bit on the reserved side, cautious almost. My sister, on the other hand, comes alive at the chance to confront another person. She has no fear. For myself, the fear of conflict has hurt my relationships when I allow it to. Conflict with people I love makes me nervous. I'm afraid to hurt them. I'm afraid they will hurt me. I'm scared to lose them. I'm afraid of the work it takes to keep them. I'm afraid of the work it takes to sometimes let go. People are unpredictable at times. That is a very real thing. People can hurt you even when they don't mean to. We are all human and we all make mistakes. No one is perfect. I can be very guarded with my heart in an attempt to protect myself. Are you quick to shut down when you could have given it a chance? Do you hold on to those who deserve nothing from you? It's important to guard your heart and there also needs to be a delicate balance. Your wall cannot protect you from ever getting hurt. When you never take a chance, you could be missing out on something good. And sometimes, it's time to let go. Whichever it is, don't be afraid to do it.

Value Gained

I'm sticking to telling people how I feel when I feel it, whether it's "I'm angry" or "I'm sorry." What I've found is that someone who truly cares about you doesn't run from that. You can handle your conflict constructively. You listen to one another, you communicate, and you never purposely hurt one another.

I suppose I learned how to "do it wrong" by watching mom and dad but I also learned how to find inner strength to walk away. I learned from my mom to have the strength to walk away when the bad outweighs the good. Even though sometimes she stayed too long, she would pick up and go without a plan. You are strong enough to start over. You're even strong enough to do it on your own if you have to, but you don't have to because you are strong enough to put effort into relationships that matter. Be ready for conflict and know when to wave the white flag.

Journal Prompt:

Who or what were your first examples of how to deal with conflict in relationships?

_____

_____

_____

_____

_____

_____

_____

_____

_____

_____

_____

_____

_____

_____

_____

_____

_____

_____

_____

_____

How do you normally deal with conflict? Do you confront it head on? Do you hold grudges? Do you hold it inside?

_____

_____

_____

_____

_____

_____

_____

_____

_____

_____

_____

_____

_____

_____

_____

_____

_____

_____

_____

_____

_____

_____

_____

How you handle conflict and communicate what you need has a lot to do with your communication style. (Which may be influenced or learned from your first examples stated above).

_____

_____

_____

_____

_____

_____

_____

_____

_____

_____

_____

_____

_____

_____

_____

_____

_____

_____

_____

You want to be assertive with your communication because you deserve to be heard and it's important to respect others too. Think of someone you have had a recent conflict with. If possible, talk to them about how you feel and start with an "I feel" statement. If you do not feel like you can talk to them, write them a letter. (Start with your "I feel" statement.)

"I feel _____ when you _____

and I need _____

_____

_____

_____

PASSIVE	ASSERTIVE	AGGRESSIVE
Soft spoken, avoiding eye contact	Good eye contact, firm voice	Bullying, threatening, loud voice, glaring
Giving in, not speaking up, not saying anything	Using an "I Feel" Statement	Demanding, loud, verbally hostile
Putting others' needs before your own	Stating your needs and emotions while respecting the needs and emotions of others as well	Putting your needs before others. Not giving thought or respect to someone else's needs and emotions

Relationship Skills II

CHAPTER 4
MY BEST FRIEND

Growing up, I never saw my mom with other women. She didn't go to brunch, hang out at the club or talk on the phone with girlfriends. I've only ever seen her with her sisters. My mom is the second oldest of six children and while I got the sense that they would help each other if needed, I never felt my mom was very close to them either. I would describe my mom as sort of a loner. My mom would later tell me that she also describes herself as a loner and considered me and my siblings' as her friends. My mother would explain that she would try to make friends at school but was continuously bullied and picked on, so she began to stick to herself. Whatever painful experiences my mom faced with other young girls as a child would continue into her adult life. If my mom would have had more female support maybe things would have been different for her. If she had had someone to share her struggles with or had someone to encourage her along the way, perhaps things would have been different for my sister and me. I don't think either of us knew how to maintain relationships with other women. How I found the beautiful soul that is my best friend is beyond me.

I met her when I was 12 years old in the 7th grade. I was a new student at a new school. My cousin went there too but of course they put us in different classes. I had heard about a bully who everyone was afraid of, even the 8th graders. Even the teachers! That was the very first day. Bad news travels fast. I don't remember who told me about the bully because I didn't know anyone. I wasn't sure I was going to like this new school. I walked into my new classroom with my brand-new FILA backpack and took a seat. At some point it was time to choose lockers and locker partners. What were the teachers thinking? I knew no one. Suddenly a girl with a huge afro puff turned to me and said, "You want to be my locker partner?" I thought she was the bully! I couldn't say no, or she would beat me up. So, I said yes. At least I had a partner. At least I wasn't the last one to be chosen. Turns out, she was not the bully, but would later tell me that she was just as nervous as I was that day. She would also tell me that her first impression was that I was rich because of my FILA backpack. As you already know, that couldn't be farther from the truth. So, we both learned a lesson that day about first impressions. The girl who I thought was the bully became my best friend. We've been rocking now for over 20 years. We've had our ups and downs but honestly, nothing I can remember worth telling. We have worked on our friendship and it has prevailed because we are intentional about making it work. Even through times of quietness, through marriages, babies, life, and everything else, we are still making it work. I wouldn't say it's a traditional friendship. We don't talk every day or post hashtag "friendship goals" pictures. We are terrible with pictures. But she gets me, always has, always will. She's still the one I would go to if I ever needed anything. And she is the person that knows the most about me. I honestly believe she's been a better friend to me than I have been to her and I'm grateful for it. I have not always shown up like I should and not because I'm not a good friend but because I sometimes didn't know how to be a good friend. I didn't really know what it meant to be there for someone else because I was too busy taking care of me. And as I mentioned before, there needs to be a balance. It's a relationship that I will always put the work into because it's a relationship I value. We've built trust and closeness over the years. You will know when it's real and worth it. You won't worry about her telling your secrets or talking about you behind your back. Time will tell. You may have to kiss a few frogs to get to the prince or the princess.

She made the unbearable days more bearable. She listened when I needed an ear. She's wiped away tears that I couldn't hold back. She has seen through tears that I've held in. She encourages me and helps me to see myself in a different light. She has stood strong even when I wavered. I followed her to high school and right to the University of Illinois to hold on to the friendship.

Value Gained

Girls are often told to be careful around other girls. We may hear "she's not your friend" or "watch her." I've heard girls say, "I don't have any close female friends", or "I only hang with boys". Relationships are essential, friendships are important. Even though my mom didn't have a lot of luck with friendships, she never pushed her fear of them onto me or my sister. We were encouraged to be friends with our peers. We are made to connect with people. I value all the relationships with the women in my life. As you continue to grow, you learn that as women we can and should build each other up. Being cautious of other women isn't necessary all the time. Having a lot of friends isn't mandatory but keep your eyes open for the real ones. Be open to those who push, encourage and support you. Cultivate those relationships. Sometimes a good friend is closer than a brother or a sister and in the words of the beautiful ballerina Misty Copeland "Anything is possible when you have the right people to support you.

Journal Prompt:

1. Choose one person that has been a good friend to you or has just been there for you when you needed someone. Write a letter telling them that you appreciate them and why. Read or give the letter to them.

_____

_____

_____

_____

_____

_____

_____

_____

_____

_____

_____

_____

_____

_____

_____

_____

_____

_____

_____

2. We are not perfect. What mistakes have you made in your life regarding a significant relationship? Did you fail to show up when you should have been there? Have you been messy in your friendships? What steps can you take to restore the friendship?

_____

_____

_____

_____

_____

_____

_____

_____

_____

_____

_____

_____

_____

_____

_____

_____

_____

_____

_____

_____

Responsible Decision Making

CHAPTER 5
THIS CANNOT BE LIFE!

I want to say that I was on the right track as a teenager, and I had my head on straight when it came to boys. The truth is, I was scared. After I saw my mother go through one crazy relationship after the next, I was terrified. I was unsure of what a healthy relationship between a man and a woman looked like. I had an idea of a model relationship from my paternal grandparents. But my up close and personal view of my parents' marriage was what I saw every day. I was also insecure with how I looked. I didn't carry the confidence needed for a healthy relationship and I certainly didn't have the maturity. My younger sister and I were complete opposites. While I was nervous, she was bold. She was confident in her appearance and adventurous in her relationships. Yet we were both ill-equipped to deal with our "young romantic relationships." I didn't want to be taken advantage of and I certainly didn't want to be distracted but that didn't stop my "first love."

I was 16 when we met at the mall and I was just surprised that anyone even wanted to talk to me. I was so insecure. And that was my first mistake. If you don't know who you are and you lack confidence in who you are, you are not ready to pair up with someone else, no matter how old you are. We didn't immediately engage in a relationship and we were friends for a while, because like I said, I was guarded, and he was not interested in breaking down my wall when there were many other girls out there. We went to prom together and eventually "fell in love" or at least I thought it was love. In 2001 I wrote:

"I had to write it down because I don't want this feeling to ever leave and I don't want to forget it."

I thought I was in deep love and I suppose it was in my 19-year-old brain. Here is what I didn't know at the time (well I had some idea): the love of my life was also the love of her life and her life. Sis, he was for everybody. I don't want to generalize all young men, but I don't feel like this is new news or something unique. We were young but I must be honest. I wasn't giving my cookies up, so he found it elsewhere. However, he told me he would wait for as long as I wanted. He said exactly what I wanted to hear so that I would become another notch on his belt. His fake patience made me wish I hadn't been such a fool. I wish my mother had told me not to be a fool. I gave away something precious in hopes of keeping this 'boy.' Believe me, the trade-off was certainly not worth it. I had convinced myself that if I had sex with my boyfriend, he would stop having sex with other girls. Was I a fool or did I believe I was in love? I thought I was in love. At the time, it was real for me. My only regret is having sex when I knew I wasn't ready, knowing I didn't want to. We all go through "first love" growing pains.

This is a time to learn about yourself, find out who you are, work to accomplish your goals, and have fun. There will always be time for boys. While he is growing and developing, you should be doing the same. How can you know what you want in a man if you don't know who you are as a woman? I may not have known exactly what I wanted but there was one idea that was already taking form and that is that I deserve better.

On April 18, 2004 I wrote:
"He can't love me like he thinks or he wouldn't let it go like this. I deserve so much better. I know it." And so do you.

What are your goals and aspirations? Do you want to go to college? Do you want to own your own business? What kind of woman do you want to be? There will always be time for boys but now is the time to get to know yourself. Sometimes, romantic relationships get in the way of that because they may come with distractions or simply emotions that you may not be ready to deal with.

Value Gained
After my dad, my mom had a few relationships but none that I remember being serious. One was immature, one was abusive, another was a cheater, none

of them helped to make her a better person. She did that on her own. I wish my mom had told me she was a fool to stay for as long as she did with those guys. I wish she had shared that sometimes we do crazy things when we think we're in love, but being in love is no reason to stay with anyone who doesn't, won't, or can't respect you. Being in love is not a reason to do things that you don't want or are not ready to do. Being in love does not erase your worth. No man should talk down to you and make you feel that you are less than what you are. No man or boy should try to get you to give up something that is the most precious thing you have – your value.

Here is another vital point about relationships: sometimes you must know when to let them go. It doesn't matter if it's family, friend, or romantic. I went from writing about how much I loved him to writing about how I couldn't believe I stayed with him for so long. So, this isn't a chapter about relationships. This is a chapter about you being responsible with yourself.

I feel that most young women don't know or understand the power we have. I once had a friend tell me that the reason why men work, get fresh, take girls out on dates is in the hopes of getting the girl! You have what they want! And it is worth more than dinner, a movie, a hairdo or a trip to the nail salon. It is worth his last name or at the very least a committed, monogamous relationship if that's what you want.

Simply put, you are worth the wait if you want to wait. If he is not willing to wait, then he is not worth it. And if you just want to have fun, that's cool too. Let him move on to the next chick willing to risk it all for some Applebee's. Remember your worth! I'm not saying he's not the love of your life, I'm just saying he may not be the love of your life. You better figure out who you are and what you want first.

Journal Prompt:

Have you ever changed who you are or given up something important to you for the sake of a relationship or another person? Why did you feel you needed to compromise yourself?

_____

_____

_____

_____

_____

_____

_____

_____

_____

_____

_____

_____

_____

_____

_____

_____

_____

_____

_____

Identify three personal goals that you have. These goals can be life goals, health goals, personal or educational. Write down three steps you need to achieve to reach that goal.

Goal One:

_____

_____

_____

_____

_____

Goal Two:

_____

_____

_____

_____

_____

Goal Three:

_____

_____

_____

_____

_____

_____

Sometimes you have to weigh the cost and benefits of a decision to determine if it is worth it. The costs are literally what you have to give up or consequences you may have to face if you make a certain decision. The benefits are what you gain. If it's going to cost you, your goals, hopes, and dreams I can guarantee it's not worth it.

What are the costs and the benefits to a tough decision you need to make?

Costs	Benefits

Self-Management II

CHAPTER 6
IT'S MOSTLY MENTAL

Another thing I am sure of is that drug use led to my mother's suicide attempt. If you ask my sister, it happened a few times. If you ask my brother, he doesn't remember it happening at all. It turns out my sister is right. It happened numerous times. My mother only recently confirmed that to me. I remember very clearly one time. My sister, my brother and I were just dropped off at home after a church function. We got out of the car, walked up the front porch stairs, rang the doorbell, and waited. I had to have been in the 5th or 6th grade. (I can kind of keep track by what house an event took place in and who was around). As we were waiting on the porch my mom opened the door, I immediately knew something was wrong. Her balance was off as she struggled to stand upright. Her eyes were unfocused as she sort of looked past us even though we were standing right in front of her. Her speech was slurred as she stumbled over her words and I couldn't quite make out what she was saying as she half smiled. I'm not quite sure how it happened but the ambulance came, and my mom ended up getting her stomach pumped because she had taken a lot of pills, in an attempt to take her own life. I'm not sure if she called 911 or if my grandfather called. Maybe I called. My mom would tell us later that she had indeed tried to take her life but that when she opened the door and saw us, she immediately regretted that decision. It was at that moment she decided she wanted to live, if not for herself, then for her children. What if we hadn't come home at that time? If we had been a moment later this might be a different story altogether.

Unfortunately, the story didn't end there. After many failed attempts at Alcoholics Anonymous, Narcotics Anonymous, and any other rehabilitation you could think of, many years would pass before either of my parents would become totally free from drugs, alcohol, and eventually even cigarettes. In fact, I was in 9th grade when my mom would enter drug rehabilitation for the last time. Here is my journal entry from March 13, 1997:

"My mom stole $35 from me. I think she may have used it to buy drugs. So, she had a relapse. She had to check into a hospital...Officer Revere took us to school Monday and is helping us out."

I remember that ride with Officer Revere to school. She drove me all the way from the west side of Chicago to the North side where I attended high school. I remember her buying me bus tokens and telling me everything would be alright. She told us we had a choice of who we would live with while my mom got better. My brother would end up with my maternal grandmother, I would live with my paternal grandmother for a while before joining my sister to live with my paternal aunt and uncle for the remainder of freshman year. My aunt and uncle had five children of their own. They weren't perfect but I will always love them for taking us in and treating us like their own.

Mental health was never a topic brought up in my household or any of my friends' households. In fact, in the Black Community, mental health and words like depression, anxiety, etc. were considered as taboo as words like gay or molestation. They were things you just didn't talk about. They were things that got swept under the rug. The problem with sweeping stuff under the carpet is, you can still see the dirt. The pile gets bigger and bigger until you are tripping over it. Not talking about something doesn't make it go away. In fact, it won't go away at all and it will rear its ugly head eventually. In our family and many other families these were just things you prayed about. Even today, I have young people from so many cultures tell me that they cannot talk to their parents about their feelings of depression and anxiety. They are afraid to talk about it with their family. In truth, 1 in 5 US adults experience mental illness and 17% of young people ages 6-17 experience mental health issues (www.nami.org). I would consider that serious and even in a day and time where there is a lot of information available and people are being encouraged to seek help, it still sometimes seems taboo. People are ashamed to say what they have been through. You are not alone. I am right there with you. I was never formally diagnosed with depression or anxiety as a young person. I never sought therapy or talked to anyone about my extreme sadness and anxiety about what was happening around me. I only wrote about it. I know that it affected me as an adult. I kept my thoughts of not being good enough, smart enough, pretty enough, just not enough to deal with everything, to myself.

August 30, 1996:
"Life is so messed up. There is too much pressure on me. I'm only 14, aren't I supposed to be enjoying life?"

August 31, 1996:
"Last night I packed my bags and said I was leaving. I had the money and everything. I just don't have the guts. "

March 13, 1997:
"Man, this week has been tough. Too much stress for a 15-year-old. But maybe, just maybe it will all work out for the best. Never expect too much."

June 11, 1997:
"Excuse me while I cry myself to sleep."

July 16, 1997:
"I'm so unhappy. I don't know why. Sometimes I'm happy, sometimes I'm not. [It's] difficult to understand."

December 15, 1997
"I think I'm going into a state of depression. I got an ED (early dismissal) from school because I couldn't find my ID which sent me into a state of emotions."

I am quite sure I was depressed. I was sad more days than not. I was feeling worthless, I wasn't able to concentrate at school some days, and I was tired and drained both physically and mentally. That, my friends, is the simple definition of clinical depression.

My mom was away getting the help she needed, and we were safe but for more than a year I wrote about how sad I was, even though I continued to wear a smile. I wish someone around me had noticed. I dealt with my sadness silently and alone. I just want you to know that I see you. If you are feeling sad more days than not, or experiencing anxiety, please seek help. If you can't talk to your parents, talk to your school social worker, school psychologist, or school counselor. They are equipped to help you cope and find resources for you and your family. If you're not in school talk to someone you can trust or your doctor. If you are experiencing feelings of loneliness, sadness, or hopelessness you may be experiencing depression. If you feel overwhelmingly stressed, can't stop your mind from racing or worry most of the time, you may be experiencing anxiety. If you even think that either of these may be an issue, please seek help immediately.

Value Gained

Now, I see my therapist whenever I need to. There is no shame in needing someone to help you work through whatever you are going through. Understanding my childhood trauma and how it affects me today helps me know who I am and allows me to move forward with my life. I can use my story to help someone else. I can recognize patterns of unhealthy thinking and correct them. I can reach out for help if I need it. There is no shame in that. Your mental health is important. It will affect your relationships with others but most importantly, it will affect your relationship with yourself. Your relationship with you is the most important one you have. There is no way you can help someone else, give to someone else, or be there for someone else if you do not take care of yourself.

Journal Prompt:

How does your family deal with mental health issues? Is it discussed in a healthy way or is it something considered secret?

_____

_____

_____

_____

_____

_____

_____

_____

_____

_____

_____

_____

_____

_____

_____

_____

_____

_____

In chapter 2 we began to talk about some ways to help you regulate your emotions. A grounding technique is something that helps you to focus on the here and now and deal with strong emotions. One of my favorite grounding techniques is the 5 4 3 2 1 technique:

5 things you can see
4 things you can touch
3 things you can hear
2 things you can smell
1 thing you can taste

I want you to google 'grounding techniques.' Pick a few, try them and write down the ones that seem to help you cope.

1. _____

2. _____

3. _____

4. Write down three affirmations or positive declarations about yourself that begin with "I am…" to encourage and remind yourself that you are capable of handling anything that comes your way. Consider writing them on a note card to carry around, or place on your mirror so that you will see them daily. Let's get you started:

1. I am valued. I am worthy. I am important and my voice matters.

2. I am _____

3. I am _____

Social Awareness

CHAPTER 7
MY SADDEST MEMORY

Very recently, I was taking part in a video podcast about mental health during the pandemic. At the end of the talk the host asked if I would participate in a "rapid fire". He would ask me questions and I would have to say the first thing that came to mind. It started easy. It began with questions like, what's my favorite hobby, movie, and drink?" He then asked me what my saddest memory is. It popped into my mind almost immediately because I know what it is. I wrote about it in my journal on August 28, 1996:

"I guess you're wondering why it took me so long to write again. It's been a full year since I last made an entry in this diary. Well last summer, I left you at grandma's house. Well now I'm back again, and it's so good to write in a diary again. I can get everything off my chest. There is so much to say…. Remember when I said I didn't care who paid for the graduation as long as both my parents showed up? Well neither one showed up and that hurt me deeply."

During my early years working as a school social worker, I worked in a k-8 elementary building in Maywood, Illinois. Every May/June was filled with celebrations for the 8th graders moving on to high school. There was a dance, a field trip, and a ribbon pinning ceremony. During the ribbon pinning ceremony, the parents would meet their graduate in the middle of the gym and pin a ribbon on them. When parents didn't show up, the classroom teacher would step in to perform the ritual. It happened sometimes and usually the kids walked back on stage smiling. It happened to a young man and I saw him search for his mom, dad, or whoever was supposed to be there.

When no one walked forward to do the honors, his 8th grade teacher did. Instead of stepping back on stage and taking his place, he ran out of the gym into the bathroom crying. My heart broke into a million pieces for him. His teacher and I followed him out of the gym to comfort him. He was me and I was him, more than 10 years later. It was my same experience. I felt like I was transported in time. I went through that entire ceremony hoping that my mom and dad would show up. My aunt and cousin came to support me. Remember, I also had a cousin I attended junior high school with. Even though I had other family there, I didn't feel like they were there for me. When I realized my parents didn't attend, I ran out of the room where we were having a reception after the ceremony with tears streaming down my face. Breathless, my best friend ran after me and helped me to calm down. I don't remember what she said but I remember wiping my tears and smiling through the pain. I went out to celebrate with her and her family.

Value Gained

It happened more than 20 years ago and it is the first story that pops into my mind when asked about my saddest memory. And one that still brings tears to my eyes. I'm teary writing this! And while it may not seem like a big deal or even the most traumatic event I've dealt with, it's the one that gets me every time. That's the thing with these experiences – you don't know how they are going to affect you. Two people can experience the same thing and have two very different perspectives. But this experience helped me to empathize with another student who experienced the same thing years later. I was able to be a light to that student because, in the words of Viktor Frankl I had "endured the burning." I know that doesn't sound like fun but your life has meaning, even the parts that hurt. It's important to find the lessons in everything and use them to help yourself. Use them to help others.

Journal Prompt:

1. Write about a time you understood something another person was going through because you had experienced something similar.

_____

_____

_____

_____

_____

_____

_____

_____

_____

_____

_____

_____

_____

_____

_____

_____

_____

_____

_____

_____

_____

2. If this hasn't happened yet, write about how a difficult situation you have dealt with can be "a light" for someone else.

_____

_____

_____

_____

_____

_____

_____

_____

_____

_____

_____

_____

_____

_____

_____

_____

_____

_____

Self-Awareness II

CHAPTER 8
FORGIVENESS

Remember when I said I never shared how I felt because I didn't want to burden others? Ok, good. I also didn't want to hurt the people I loved by expressing how they hurt me. My initial hesitation to answer the question about my saddest memory was because I had never told my mom or dad how much them not attending my 8th grade graduation had hurt me. I'm not sure we ever talked about it but as you know, I wrote about it. Well, my mom happened to be watching the Facebook live and she saw that part particularly, the part where I talked about my saddest memory. She called me the next day to apologize. She told me that even through the screen she could sense my hurt. Twenty years later, my mom apologized for not attending my 8th grade graduation.

I'll share with you another tidbit that came out in therapy at some point. I'm sitting there in tears with my therapist and I'm not sure what he asked me, but it had to be somewhere along the lines of, "Do you ever talk about it?" Without thinking I said, "What's the point in saying anything if it's not going to change anything?" I was stunned that those words came out of my mouth and I think my therapist was also shocked. My eyes went wide at the realization of what I had just revealed about myself. I know a lot of people feel that way too. I believe that's why Baldwin's quote that "Nothing can change until it is faced" speaks volumes to me. I wasn't facing problems if I didn't think they would change but if you remember the beginning of the quote, "not everything that is faced can be changed." When you can't change it, you learn to cope by writing, talking, and focusing on you. Sometimes, the hurt cannot be changed, so you forgive.

Forgiveness is a choice. It is intentional, and you hold all the power. You get to choose if you forgive someone. You literally make a conscious and deliberate decision to say, "I forgive you and I'm letting this go. I'm moving on." It is you saying I will not let this situation stop me from being great. I won't keep thinking about it and use it as an excuse. Forgiveness is purposeful. You must forgive someone on purpose and then remember that you have forgiven them repeatedly. You see, forgiveness doesn't mean you forget, in fact you remember, and you remember well. You learn from it; you grow from it, but you remind yourself that you will not let unforgiveness hold you back. If you go into this thinking that you will change someone else, you will be disappointed every time. All you have control over is you.

So, to answer my own question, "What's the point in saying anything if it's not going to change anything?" I was the point. I am the point. You are the point.

Value Gained

Forgiveness sets you free! I didn't need my mother's apology because I forgave her long ago. I had chosen to forgive her because (1) I love her and most importantly, (2) I needed to be able to keep moving forward. What if I had chosen to hold on to that hurt? What if I decided I wasn't going to go to high school because no one seemed to care about 8th grade? We sometimes let these experiences hold us back like that. We use them as excuses to stop our growth. I understood that sometimes people hurt us. Let the person's action's guide you in deciding if they are worth the effort of a relationship after you've healed from the offense.

Since my junior year of high school, my mom has spent her life devoted to her three children and I believe, trying to make it all up to us. She answers every time we call. She will give us anything we ask for within her power and she's an awesome grandmother to all of her grandchildren. She has become my greatest cheerleader and my biggest supporter. Even if she hadn't done all of that, I still chose to forgive her. Though teary eyed from time to time, I wasn't going to waste time being angry with my mom. Her actions afterward told me I could trust her with our relationship.

Journal Prompt:

1. Write a letter to someone you need to forgive. Begin with how you feel, talk about how they hurt you and why you are hurt. You don't need to share the letter with the person unless you want to.

_____

_____

_____

_____

_____

_____

_____

_____

_____

_____

_____

_____

_____

_____

_____

_____

_____

2. Now talk/write about your plan to take back your power to begin to forgive, heal, and move on.

_____

_____

_____

_____

_____

_____

_____

_____

_____

_____

_____

_____

_____

_____

_____

_____

_____

Self-Management III

CHAPTER 9
GRANDMA'S GIRL: GRIEF

I often talk about how I pulled myself up by my own bootstraps, but the truth is a part of the resilience I've been able to portray comes from having people in my corner. I don't mean this in a romantic way. I mean this in a healthy relationship way. I've talked about my bestie and how that relationship developed but long before she came along, my father's mother was there for me. My grandmother was "the one." Sometimes, you just need one person to believe in you, one person who listens to you to help you to make it through. It could be a family member, a friend, someone at school or at work, or even your higher power. Your one reminds you that even on the worst days, everything will be okay. Most importantly, long after they're gone, you'll always remember how they made you feel. Their strength strengthens you even if they couldn't or can't whisk you away from whatever problem you're facing.

My mother had the same relationship with her grandmother and to hear her talk about it now, you can hear the love and admiration in her voice for the woman she sees as a second mother. I had the privilege of watching them together and I could see how my great grandmother cared for my mother. Their relationship was special and different from that of her other siblings. I believe that's why my mother always encouraged my relationship with my grandmother. She was never jealous of it. She never tried to keep me from her. She knew how important time together is once you've found "the one."

My mother also loved my grandmother even after she and my dad divorced. She always spoke of her mother in law with love and grandma spoke the same of her. That's the type of woman she was. She was full of love.

For me and many others she was a real-life guardian angel. I'm not sure how grandmothers have that ability, but they do. I am who I am today because of her. She dropped so much wisdom into me I could never tell it all. I think it's how I was able to stay sane and keep moving. I wanted to make her proud. I mostly learned by watching her. She loved hard and often gave too much (in my opinion). She might also curse you out one minute (because you needed to be told) and show you love the next. Everyone loved her. She would often tell me the story of how she fell in love with me from that moment she laid eyes on me. She told me she made a promise to take care of me and she kept that promise. She had almost 20 grandchildren, a host of nieces and nephews and so many others who referred to her as grandma or Aunt Gussie. She managed to make us each feel special in our own way. I was her favorite though. People may not want to admit it but it's true and I ain't here to argue about it – this is my book.

Value Gained

When she died, I felt such incredible grief and guilt. I had grief for what I had lost and guilt because I didn't feel like I had lived up to her expectations. It wasn't like I hadn't lost anyone before but those losses couldn't compare to losing "my one." We had lost grandpa (her husband) more than 20 years prior, but this was the first time I felt as though I really had to deal with grief. I didn't think I would come back from this hurt. I'll be honest, it still hurts and it's been about three years. It doesn't hurt as much and most days are good. But every now and then, I still cry. I regret not taking care of her the same way she had taken care of me and the guilt is a different kind of pain.

I never saw my mother deal with grief up close. She avoids funerals like the plague. But when asked, she reflects fondly on her grandmother and keeps a set of dishes that once belonged to her. I know how I felt when my grandmother died so I can only imagine that she felt the same. What I learned is that grief is a process. Some days are more bittersweet than others but each day is a little better.

It's important to grieve your loss properly. Whether that means crying or screaming, it's important to get it out. All of the important things about using your voice matter even in grief. Identify your sadness, your anger, or your guilt. And when you're ready, move into acceptance – accept that what has happened cannot be changed. How do we move on? You may have to reimagine your life without the person. Your life will continue to grow around your grief. In true Ava form I wrote my grandma a letter – telling her how much I loved her and that while I was sad to see her go, I was happy that she would no longer suffer and would be reunited with loved ones. In the midst of my guilt I had to realistically think about what my grandmother would really say to me. Even when she was disappointed she still expressed her love for me and how proud she was of me, so that is what I held on to. I was able to let go of my guilt because I knew her and I knew she would not want me to feel that way.

Sometimes grief isn't the loss of a person. Sometimes it's the loss of a relationship, the loss of health, a job, or a home. No matter the loss, it hurts, and you have to give yourself time to grieve before accepting the loss and creating your "new normal".

Journal Prompts:

1. How have you processed loss or grief in your life? What have you learned in the process?

_____

_____

_____

_____

_____

_____

_____

_____

_____

_____

_____

_____

_____

_____

_____

_____

_____

_____

2. Write about a situation you wished you would have handled differently. Maybe you feel sad, angry or ashamed at the way you handled it. Ask yourself: "Would your "one" hold this against you? What advice would they give you?

_____

_____

_____

_____

_____

_____

_____

_____

_____

_____

_____

_____

_____

_____

_____

_____

_____

_____

_____

_____

Self-Management IV

CHAPTER 10
GRATEFUL

This entire chapter is a value gained. I have learned to look for the small positive things in any situation. Sometimes things suck and that's a fact. Our brains are wired to focus on the things we need to learn to keep us safe. *Unfortunately,* that usually isn't the positive fun stuff. It's usually the stuff that makes us scared or anxious or sad. That doesn't mean we only focus on that. We must focus our thoughts on the good things, however small, and however difficult they may be to find.

My mom is the queen of letting things go and being grateful. So, I am sure I learned that trick from her. You've read about only a fraction of what my mom has been through, from abusive relationships to overcoming drug addiction and battles with her mental health. I never heard her complain, blame, or shame anyone – not a single person.

I am so grateful for every experience I have had in my life. Without them I would not be who I am, and I am in a place where I can honestly say that I am happy with myself.

Each experience has helped me help someone else. It's no coincidence, that I chose a job in the helping profession. Over the years I have met several students from preschool on up who have a similar story to mine.

When I can comfort a student, who watched her mom overdose because I know personally how that feels. I am grateful that I'm not just another adult talking. I'm an adult who truly understands. There's a lot I haven't shared in this book, but my goal of being open is to let someone know that they can overcome the hard times. Life was tough but I am thankful to be alive.

Melody Beattie (The Language of Letting Go, 1990) said that "gratitude unlocks the fullness of life. It turns what we have into enough, and more. It turns denial into acceptance, chaos to order, confusion to clarity. It can turn a meal into a feast, a house into a home, a stranger into a friend. It turns problems into gifts, failures into successes, the unexpected into perfect timing, and mistakes into important events. It can turn an existence into a real life, and confusing situations into important and beneficial lessons. Gratitude makes sense of our past, brings peace for today, and creates a vision for tomorrow."

I thank God for sending people in my life who helped me along the way. I am thankful for my best friend who came when I needed her and was reliable from day one even when I wasn't. I appreciate her encouragement through the years and her words that always let me know that anything is possible. I love her truth when I need to be told about myself, gently. I'm grateful for my grandmother who taught me to be loving and kind and an example of boldness and bravery. I'm grateful for shopping trips and school supplies. I am thankful that even through the worst of times we never went hungry. Grandpa always came through with groceries and a smile. I'm grateful for my aunt and uncle who took in kids that were not their own but never treated us differently. I'm thankful for my aunt sitting and teaching me my very first song for Sunday service and for telling me I'm beautiful when I didn't believe I was. I'll never forget the time they came up with money for my majorette uniform freshman year when I knew they didn't have it.

I'm grateful for the teacher who told me I had a beautiful smile long before I ever knew braces were a possibility.

I'm grateful for my parents. I wouldn't be who I am without their story and I like me.

I guess I learned a lot about how not to do things by watching mom, but she also taught me perseverance and I am grateful for that. It's because of her I have this "get up and go spirit." Even when things were hard, she didn't give up. She tried her best. I can't imagine what those tough times I've talked about must have been like for her. She has taught me not to let trauma stop me and to think on good things. She taught me that it's never too late to turn it around. It's never too late to be there for the people you care about. She's taught me how to show up for the people you love. She hasn't missed a single milestone since that 8th grade graduation. She never tells me "no." She has shown me that I can depend on her. She encourages me like no other. She often tells me how proud she is of me and tells everyone about her "big girl." I'm so proud of her and everything she has become, and I look forward to all the things she will tell me and for that I am grateful.

Journal Prompt:

1. How can an attitude of gratitude help you to "make sense of our past, bring peace for today, and create a vision for tomorrow?" Name three things and/or people in your life that you are grateful for and why.

_____

_____

_____

_____

_____

_____

_____

_____

_____

_____

_____

_____

_____

_____

_____

_____

_____

_____

CONCLUSION

The ancient Greek philosopher Socrates said that *"An unexamined life is not worth living."* We are a continual work in progress. I am not where I want to be, but I am so grateful for the journey to find my way. If we are not stopping along the way to examine who we are, where we are, and where we want to be, what are we doing? It doesn't mean that you can't be happy with where you are. It means that we never stop growing.

Our circumstances do not dictate our value. If there is one thing I want you to walk away with, it is that you have value. That value is second nature to you. You were born with it. It cannot be taken away from you by anyone or anything. It can't even be taken away by you. Even if you don't believe it, you still have value. You deserve the absolute best. Begin to treat yourself like you do. Be honest about how you feel. You deserve to be heard. There are some things you can change and other things that you must deal with. Change what you can and learn to cope with what you can't. Remember you are strong enough to face them all. Value relationships that encourage you and help you see yourself and get rid of relationships that make you feel less than. Forgive, every time - not for the sake of the other person but your own sake.

Your life can be a light for someone else. Everything that you experience and every choice you make helps to define who you will become. Your life is determined by the continual choices made, not the mistakes but the conscious efforts to do and be better. As Aristotle said, *"We are what we repeatedly do. Excellence, then, is not an act, but a habit."* I have shared a lot about my mom. For the last 20 years she has been repeatedly excellent, and an example that it is truly about how you finish, not how you start.

You don't have to feel the weight of your past on you. It's never too late to unlearn the harmful things we learned to protect ourselves. We won't always get it right but we live to try again.